Winning

with

Private Equity

by

Paul Anthony Thomas

Investor & Registered Investment Advisor

PO Box 2677, Abilene, Tx 79604

Paul A. Thomas

has been an active private equity investor, manager and advisor for over 20 years. He has weathered many market cycles, from complete depressions through recovery of entire market sectors. Today, he runs money for individual clients in Private Equity Funds through his advisory firm Farpoint Private Equity Advisors and Managers. Mr. Thomas is the editor of *Human Psychology in the Stock Market*; *Successful Real Estate Investing in the 1990s*; and *Supertrends® for Investors*. He authored *Winning with Private Equity.*

Mr. Thomas' direct experience includes:

- Land Development
- Infrastructure Development
- Residential & Commercial Real Estate
- Oil & Gas Exploration and Production
- Manufacturing
- The Environment
- Recycling
- Disaster Recovery and Relief
- Hospitality
- Publishing
- Government contracting
- Restaurant and Food Service
- Farming and Ranching
- Alternative Energy Generation (Co-Generation)
- Mining of Natural Resources
- Options, Futures, Commodities & Stock Markets
- Film & Video
- Waste Management
- Transportation

Investing is totally about Psychology!

EP Thomas, PhD
"Human Psychology and the Stock Market"
Bruno's Press ■ 1969.

This book is dedicated to my father,

E.P. Thomas, Ph.D.

one of the most savvy and knowledgeable

value investors and

private equity managers

I have ever known.

Order this book online at www.trafford.com/08-1176
or email orders@trafford.com

Most Trafford titles are also available at major online book retailers.

Note for Librarians: A cataloguing record for this book is available from Library and Archives Canada at www.collectionscanada.ca/amicus/index-e.html

ISBN: 978-1-4251-8675-3

We at Trafford believe that it is the responsibility of us all, as both individuals and corporations, to make choices that are environmentally and socially sound. You, in turn, are supporting this responsible conduct each time you purchase a Trafford book, or make use of our publishing services. To find out how you are helping, please visit www.trafford.com/responsiblepublishing.html

Our mission is to efficiently provide the world's finest, most comprehensive book publishing service, enabling every author to experience success. To find out how to publish your book, your way, and have it available worldwide, visit us online at www.trafford.com/10510

www.trafford.com

North America & international
toll-free: 1 888 232 4444 (USA & Canada)
phone: 250 383 6864 • fax: 250 383 6804
email: info@trafford.com

The United Kingdom & Europe
phone: +44 (0)1865 487 395 • local rate: 0845 230 9601
facsimile: +44 (0)1865 481 507 • email: info.uk@trafford.com

10 9 8 7 6 5 4 3 2

Contents

A Little History

> **Man is the sum of his past.**
> *William Faulkner*

This statement is the underlying truth for every person, successful or not. It is particularly true for people who make their living through investments. Your past history as an investor dictates what you do on a daily basis, the decisions you make, the successes and failures you have. Once you learn to control your fears and recognize your strengths, you are well on the way to being an excellent and successful private equity investor.

This book is designed to pass on lessons that have been learned during 80 years of private equity investing, fundraising and money management. Because of my upbringing, education and personality, my goal in life is to locate and participate in the greatest legal investments in the world. Many of the stories in this text were passed on to me by the experiences of my father, E.P. Thomas, PhD, a very active private equity investor. These experiences were told and re-told to me many times during the 20 years my father mentored me in the investment business. You will find some of these stories very funny, and others of them heart-wrenching.

My father, Emil Paul (E.P.) Thomas, Ph.D., was born October 25, 1913 near Boise, Idaho. His mother was a young local woman and my grandfather a handsome first-generation Basque merchant from the north of Spain. They had two children, my father and his younger sister Winifred Katherine.

Starting in about 1923, my father mowed vacant lots with a push mower to earn money. He reached what I call his “age of awakening” very early in life. The age of awakening is when a person decides that there are better ways to live life than toiling away digging ditches and hoeing cotton. The hard labor involved with his mowing tasks caused him to begin seeking other ways to support his mother and sister during the harsh times of the early 1920s. He discovered investing and higher education.

Dad saved money and purchased his first common stock in 1926, about the time that Charles Dow and his partner Edward Jones began daily publication of the Dow-Jones 30 Stock Index and the Dow-Jones Utility Index.

His initial stock investment was General Electric, a company with a strong growth history and huge potential based on the expansion of the country. My father also found the Victor Talking Machine company an interesting and novel investment opportunity. This company made devices that recorded sound and re-played those recordings. My father saw great potential in this technology.

America in the early-1920s had it rough. It was the era of Prohibition. A fierce flu epidemic had devastated the U.S. World War I had been a terrible experience, and bond defaults were relatively high.

By 1926, things were looking up. Investor confidence was strong, the "Roaring 20s" were in full swing, complete with the flappers, bathtub gin, and a new invention called television. The general public was buying stocks on credit by the truckload.

My father told me it was during these days that he decided, *if your shoe shine boy gives you a stock tip, it is time to sell.*

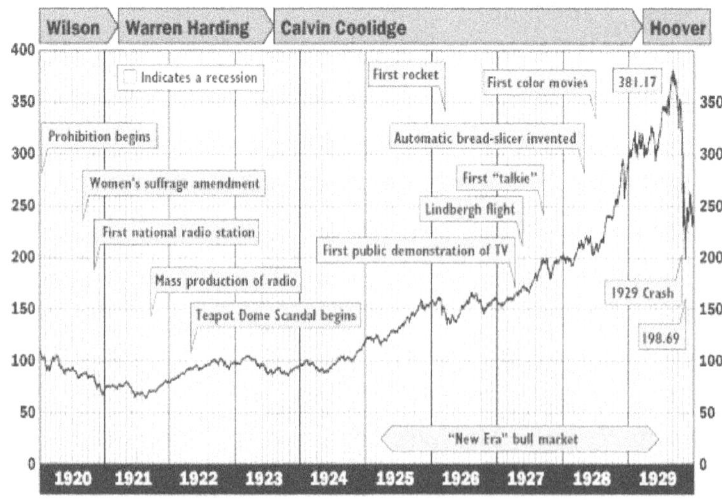

Chart © Dow Jones & Company

He also came to realize three basic rules of investing which are just as viable today as in 1926:

1. *the money is made when you purchase an investment,*
2. *the profits are not harvested until you sell that investment, and*
3. *knowing when to sell is the KEY.*

Through his experience, his stories, and his advice, my father taught me a great deal about investing. Now I have experiences of my own and lessons learned during 30 years of investing, a few of which I recount here.

Hopefully, you will gain insight and wisdom from our hard-knocks and experiences that will help you as you move forward on the road of successful investing. It is my dream that I can assist you in finding and funding the highest quality, investment opportunities and more importantly, in recognizing and rejecting poor investments that pass your way.

Perhaps you have a story to tell about a good or bad investment. I'd love to hear from you with the details.

If you would like to talk with me about topics in this book, your own experiences, my current activities, or opportunities we have uncovered during our research, please feel free to contact me.

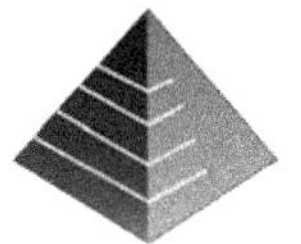

Paul A. Thomas
Farpoint Private Equity Advisors & Managers
PO Box 2677, Abilene, Texas 79604
558 Ambler Avenue, Abilene, Texas 79601
www.farpointadvisors.com
325.695.1329

Missed Opportunities

Lessons Learned the Hard Way

I love my work, but I have certainly had my share of bumps and bruises along the way. Experiences I wouldn't have missed for all the tea in China, but that I am very happy never to repeat.

I had a college buddy who was a real talker. He was down-to-earth, truthful, kind, funny, and a true friend.

In class one day, he began telling me a story of an oil well in a pasture near my home town, in an area where I was working to find oil. He knew the landowner personally. For several class periods, he kept me updated on the farmer, his wife, and their well-bore that was leaking oil to the surface. I half-listened and was entertained.

After about three weeks, I decided to take an hour-long drive to see this farm. I met the couple who told me that, the week before, they had leased their mineral rights to an interested party for $5000. They kindly let me see the pasture and, sure enough, there was a pool of fresh, green crude oil on the ground which had leaked from this abandoned oil well.

If you are actively in the market for a Private Equity investment, investigate every reasonable lead regardless of the source.

Within a year, there were 15 oil wells on this 640 acre farm, producing as much as 500 barrels per day each from a depth of less than 2000 feet.

I should have listened. My inaction cost me millions.

Another lament I have is not gathering the resources to participant in several growth opportunities where I was in on the ground floor and available, but didn't have the foresight or vision to see what was happening around me. I think of this as the "young and stupid" portion of my career.

A prime example of this is the real estate market in College Station, Texas in the late 1970's. In 1975, I entered college at Texas A&M University in College Station. I had in mind to be an oceanographer like Jacques Cousteau, but organic chemistry quickly changed my mind.

When I began school, there were 12,000 students and a total city population around 20,000. You could drive from one end of town to the other in five minutes, even with traffic. There weren't more than a dozen traffic lights.

I left College Station in 1979. By this time, the school had over 25,000 students (tremendous growth that has not been seen since) and the town was approaching 50,000 in population due, in large part, to an oil boom taking place in the area.

Sustained Growth = Profit

Although the town and school populations had both doubled in size in four short years, I was too inexperienced and dim-witted to know that a perfect storm in growth was taking place around me, making millionaires daily. I had not learned that a situation like this presents tremendous financial opportunities that are very rare indeed.

Real estate has boomed in the College Station marketplace for three decades, and I have yet to make a dollar off of this phenomena. The town has literally tripled in physical size. Also I have yet to see another market that has matched this sustained growth rate and value increase in such a short period of time, including the inflated housing boom of 2000-2007 in the U.S.

In the past 30 years, I have only seen a few other areas grow at such a break-neck pace and, believe me, when I see this happening, I do everything within my power to participate.

Examples of similar growth have happened a few times in the past 10 years along the US/Mexico border in towns like Laredo and Brownsville. Other Texas towns have seen strong growth as well, including San Marcos, Pearland, Manvel, Roundrock, Friendswood, Southlake and Keller, to mention a few. We have ongoing investment activities in most of these areas, where sustained growth can be seen and supported into the future.

In the early parts of the 21st century, Texas is generally unaffected by the market turmoil of 2008. Texas is a steady growth marketplace, returning over 25% annually to the savvy investor.

One valuable lesson that was learned during this time was "*Oil Booms Create Wealth*". When the Austin Chalk oil play hit Southeast Texas, jobs were plentiful, and people were amazed at the amount of money that followed.

When your experience tells you something looks interesting, do not hesitate, take action. Research the target until you come to a conclusion that makes sense. Your research will pay off in the investments that you uncover.

In a small town, the county seat of a rural county, there was a small 10-room motel. When the oil boom struck, this motel was always full, with people waiting for a room.

An astute businessman recognized a need and a niche. He quickly gathered the money and built a 60-room motel at the busiest intersection in the county. Within a year, he had recouped his equity investment, plus a very handsome profit. The motel continued to throw off stellar cash-flow for over a decade, and still makes money today. The owner once told me that was the greatest investment he had ever made, returning more than his original investment in cash every year into his bank account.

This story brings to mind one of my favorite historic entrepreneurs, Conrad Hilton. During the Texas oil booms of the 1920s and 1930s, he visited the small town of Cisco, Texas, and noticed that there was no place to sleep because all the existing boarding houses were full with waiting lists.

Mr. Hilton immediately took action. He rented a large building and, with the help of his family and a few investors, outfitted the building as a hotel and began selling bed space in 8-hour shifts. The hotel was filled 24-hours a day, 7 days a week.

His insightful action started Mr. Hilton toward a lifetime of excellent investments and personal prosperity.

In 1980, another example of loss by inaction was the Romney Oil Field of Eastland County, Texas.

After completing college, I was beginning to learn the nuances of geology and the oil and gas business, under the tutelage of my father. I was spending eight hours a day at a drafting table, looking at oil well logs, trying to uncover reasons to drill wildcat wells. I was prospecting. All-in-all, extremely boring work for a freshly graduated eager young man.

For one long month, I worked a 20-square-mile area. One evening, I came across a log that had all the characteristics of an overlooked oil well. I carefully worked around this log for several weeks, before showing the research to my father.

He looked at me sharply and asked, "How long have you been working on this"? I replied, "About three weeks."

First thing the next day, we headed for the county records to see if the land around this well had been leased. Turns out, 10 days before our inquiry, another geologist working the area had recorded a mineral lease on the available lands, cutting us out of what became a $100,000,000 oil discovery known as the Romney Oil Field.

Again, ignorance and inaction had cost me millions.

Inaction = Opportunity Lost

The Case for Private Equity

Consistently, throughout my 30 years and the 50 years of value investing by my mentor, the success stories that we have to share, time and time again, center on private investors who ventured into the world of business with a good management team, adequate capital and a sound idea. All of the companies listed on the world's stock exchanges are a result of some visionary leader who had a stable of investors who believed in his talent and the idea. They all have their roots in the world of private equity.

More than any other group, the startup team of investors and managers are the people who truly win in the world of investing. They are also the group with the highest failure rate. This is what makes private equity investing such a fun and exciting world. Equity investors and managers see things before other, more traditional investors. They see things that others do not and have the foresight to take advantage of what they see.

You may remember the top man at IBM saying "I see the world demand for the microcomputer to be ONE". What a near sighted statement from a man who was supposed to have vision.

Bill Gates started Microsoft with an idea, a dream, and a team of technicians who did not know the first thing about marketing. They worked their way to the position they are in today following a vision for success that no one in the established marketplace shared. Along the way, they picked up some investors who believed in what they were doing and provided management and marketing skills as well as capital.

When Microsoft went public, all of the original investors and principals won big, receiving at least 100 times their initial investment in less than 10 years time. In the private equity investing world, this is a wonderful home run.

In the middle of the last century, Trammel Crow noticed a trend in the demand for marketing and distribution facilities in the south central U.S. He saw that literally hundreds of company reps were coming into the Dallas marketplace annually to sell to the regional retail business community without a place to show and sell their goods. He built and managed the Dallas Market Center complex which eventually included several large hotels, wholesale centers and support facilities.

It was a phenomenal success. He parlayed those investments into hundreds of thousands of square feet of manufacturing and distribution space and further into a vast fortune with properties owned and managed in every major market. Do you believe that he would have ever been successful without the proper private equity investors backing his efforts?

Many investors thought he was insane; no one would ever use the massive space he had built.

But his team knew that the vision was accurate and that the program would be a tremendous success.

Shortly after opening, the Market Center was totally booked with over 1 million visitors annually. This type of success cannot happen without private equity investors.

In 1999, my real estate group saw the market developing for an upscale hotel in several Texas cities. Plans were hatched, buildings were designed, and land was purchased. Seven years later, several of these markets have increased the number of hotel rooms in the marketplace by over 30%, proving that our foresight was accurate. We were ahead of our time and many of these markets still exist and still need upscale hospitality properties.

I have a high school acquaintance that started a medical billing and service company in 1998 with $1,000,000 in capital gathered from family and investors. In 2006, his company sold for $4 billion to a major international player. In less than 10 years, each of the initial investors walked away with $1 billion in profits on an investment of $250,000.

Berkshire Hathaway® and Warren Buffet follow this style of investing. In 2006, they uncovered an Israeli company who was one of the best at what they did. This company had grand plans to expand their core product line into the Far East in support of the massive infrastructure growth in that area. This was a clean, simple idea and Mr. Buffet saw the opportunity and acted, with an initial investment of $4 billion.

He expects grand things from this investment over the next decade, and I'm going to be watching. Mr. Buffet does not participate in "boom" and "bust" type markets. He buys and builds core businesses using his experience and the talents of others, and he makes money, and I mean REAL MONEY with average returns throughout his career of over 20% on invested equity annually.

These are the types of returns I wish for my partners and the types of market plays that we research, uncover and participate in daily.

Taking Action = High Returns

Defining the Private Equity Investor

My father and I were once privileged to spend a significant amount of time with the legendary oil tycoon, H.L. Hunt. They had a detailed and candid discussion about his success as an equity investor and I listened intently.

Mr. Hunt said, "I understand my investments, like finding oil. I understand how that works, how it is made, how it is found, how it is processed, and how it is sold. If I don't understand what we are doing, I don't do it."

An interesting thing about Mr. Hunt and most successful private equity investors, they always use the term "we" in their discussions, because they work as a member of a very competent team. It was Mr. Hunt's team of advisors that were finding oil, not H.L.by himself.

He found the right people and provided the necessary tools for success. This is what private equity investing is all about.

He was the pockets behind his endeavors. If things went wrong, he was there to clean up the mess and take the loss. If things went well, everyone associated with the program made a profit.

This is the way straightforward private equity investors strive to work.

What are private equity investors like?

It's my experience that individuals who invest private equity for a living are generally very confidential people. They hold their information close. It is often difficult to understand what a private investor does for a living. They will often take on the persona of their latest project, that of a real estate investor, perhaps, or a fast-food business owner, when in reality, they own interests in many businesses in many varied sectors.

An individual that has all his wealth tied up in a fast food restaurant or chain of restaurants would be one type of investor, but generally speaking, someone who makes his living as a "private equity investor" does not hold his entire portfolio in one business, maybe one business sector, but not just one business.

Private equity investors are sometimes viewed as rude, crazy, idiotic, arrogant, or fanatical. In reality, as a rule, private equity investors are extremely conservative. They are passionate and confident. They are very diligent about their investment programs. They take few risks and are able to identify risk quickly and avoid it where possible. When you discuss something they have an interest in, they are usually exceptionally well educated and have a good grasp of the topic.

When you discuss something that they do not have a passing interest in, they quickly appear board and will move on to more interesting topics.

What does a private equity investor *really* do for a living?

Private equity investors I have known generally use the Mosaic Theory to organize their investments. They combine personal knowledge with market research. Using information from multiple sources and the experience of others, they determine whether the investment makes sense and will make money.

Private Equity Investors are generally "big picture" people who see where the product or service can go, given the proper resources.

When a Private Equity Investor takes on a project, she quickly learns what type of resources it will take to succeed. Most Private Investors desire to add more to the mix than just money, but she also understands that often, the only thing that the management team needs is capital.

Many private equity investors will not invest unless they can add value to the mix. Unless they can have a direct influence upon the success of the investment, other than a cash infusion, they are not interested. I find this approach to be very near sighted, but many Private Equity investors are this way.

On the other hand, there are private investors who just like to push money around and have the teams they invest in bring all the tools required for success. My firm falls into the latter group. We find good ideas, put teams together or find existing teams that need capital, then we invest and let the experts use our financial resources to make money.

Will I See You In The Morning?

I have a friend, who in the 1990s became entangled with a so called equity investor who later turned out to be a speculator/promoter in disguise. My friend wanted to build a business around the purchase and sale of energy assets in a very select niche of the business.

My friend was the lead accountant and front man for an oil and gas exploration company for over eight years and analyzed and executed transactions in this niche on a daily basis. He knew the competition and what type of value there was for the taking. He well understood what it would take to run the company, find the acquisitions, and manage the business. He also knew that, out of the 20 companies he was responsible for at his place of employment, the company that held these types of assets took the least amount of time to operate and was far and away the most profitable under his control.

In his search for an equity partner, he came across an individual who called himself an equity investor. Cory was a well-to-do, young man who had inherited a substantial amount of money.

My friend liked his enthusiasm and took this man into his confidence. My friend showed him the plan and explained how it was to be executed. Cory agreed to front a small amount of money, less than $10,000, and provide his balance sheet to get the company started. In return, he would receive a large ownership position in the company. My friend decided to take his offer.

The idea was sound and the business grew at an astounding pace through my friend's efforts, management skills, and vision. This company started out with nothing and in two years had 13 employees and was making net cash profits of over $200,000 per month, with virtually no equity investment, only debt.

Regrettably, the price of petroleum declined below any forecast. The company was forced to sell of all the assets and close.

What was really poor about the behavior of the so-called investor was that one Monday, when it was evident the company was in financial trouble and the fun was over, my friend came into the office to discover the partner's office was empty. Lo and behold, the speculator was gone, along with furniture, fixtures, and most of the profits.

Even though he had made over 100 times his original investment in two years' time, Cory secretly departed during the weekend and taking with him his original equity capital, plus a sizeable amount of profits. At this point in time, it was obvious that Cory was a speculator, a partner only through the good times.

In the beginning of a new venture, it is very difficult to tell who has the fortitude to see the venture through difficult times, unless they have done it before.

Cory left my friend with virtually no working capital as the company faltered. Needless to say, this situation escalated to be very ugly very quickly, but my friend stuck it out, faced all the creditors, and settled all accounts. He was the true private equity investor and certainly not a speculator or promoter.

The last we heard of Cory, he was selling real estate in Peru and I am sure, looking for his next plump pigeon.

Consider

- The inventor
- The promoter/speculator
- The private equity investor

What are the differences between inventing, investing and speculating? The distinction lies in motivation, psychology, knowledge and attitude. And once you discern which a person is, using the correct terminology is critical for you to appear knowledgeable and educated in the world of private equity.

An **inventor** likes to make things or provide services, but generally knows a marginal amount about the overall market or the players. He will know his direct competition, his local customer base, but he doesn't truly understand what it would take to make his product or service a widespread success (unless, like Ron Popiel of the legendary company RonCo®, he has done it before). If he has executed on a product or service successfully before, he would fall more into the category of a private equity investor, not just an inventor. If the inventor understands all it takes to complete the task of marketing something he has designed and manufactured, then he is much more in touch with what will be required to be successful. At that point, his investment in the new product is just that, a private investment in a new product for his company to make and market.

Calling a true private equity investor a speculator or promoter is like calling the most renowned heart surgeon in the world a quack. It is a terrible insult.

During the creation of his invention or service, the inventor will learn many details, but rarely does he fully comprehend the scope of where the product or program will make or lose money; what type of management or caliber of investment will be necessary to make the product or service something others will want to purchase.

Often inventors are called entrepreneurs. Generally they can take a company or product to a certain level, but no further. They aren't comfortable relinquishing control or having others make money from their ideas.

I admire these individuals; they are what make America great. Our world could not function without these risk takers and the United States would not be the most powerful nation in the world without their "I can do anything" spirit.

Inventor	**Private Equity Investor**	**Speculator Promoter**
Expert on Product or Service	Is an authority on the product or service	Knows little about product
Builds/provides services	Committed to Success	Committed to his profits
Wins if his inventions work or services are used.	Wins if all parties are successful and make money.	Wins if there is no trouble along the way to profits.
Creator	Market maker	Trader
Life savings	Large investment %	Small investment %
Knows a few players	Knows key players	Knows Pigeons
No Plan B	Solid Plan B	What is Plan B?
Relies on his creativity and imagination	Relies on known quantities	Relies on others
He wins and some others may win.	Everyone wins	He cares only if HE wins.

A **speculator/promoter** is generally a salesman. He takes a cursory review of what someone else is offering (a program or a service) and decides he is going to get on board and sell the product/service. Speculators listen to the news and popular opinion, then make an investment decision, hoping that their sources don't lead them astray. He rarely can reproduce the product or service because he does not take the time to learn the nuances of the business.

The salesman/promoter will generally admit they have little idea about the inner workings of the company. Speculators often don't fully understand what the company does to make money. You would be hard pressed to find a speculator in the commodities markets that knows all the uses for a soy bean or what it takes to grow a profitable stand of corn.

The speculator relies totally on the expertise and hard work of others. If the company fails, he is not at great financial risk, nor is he going to be around to deal with the aftermath of business closure.

On the other hand, a **private equity investor will generally** choose to become an authority in the areas of her investments. She wants to understand what her money is buying. She will understand the science behind the product.

She will deeply research the marketplace. She will know the niche that the product fills. She will know the competition, often on a very friendly basis. She will have a mentor to advise her on the various aspects of selling the product or service.

She will have the ability to arrange needed financing and place necessary cash into the endeavor.

Some private equity investors like to build companies from the ground up (like Herb Kelleher, founder of Southwest Airlines). Others prefer building companies after someone else has uncovered a profitable niche and needs capital to fully exploit that opportunity.

Tricks to Winning With Your Investments

Once I consulted with a company who had a wonderful safety product with numerous uses in many different markets. This company had contracts in hand from foreign governments to purchase thousands of dollars worth of the product line. Unfortunately, this company lacked the capital to manufacture and deliver the finished product to receive payment.

This company tried factoring their contracts, but since the contracts were foreign, they did not have success. All they needed was $500,000 in capital to proceed to the success table with markets throughout the US and abroad.

Their margins were high, well over 100%, but three critical factors kept them from success. They had a dysfunctional management team who was exceptionally greedy, they were hamstrung by analysis and “image building”, and they were undercapitalized.

The company floundered and the investors, who put up millions to develop the product, lost their entire outlay, just because the management team could not focus on the task at hand, cash-flow.

Avoiding pitfalls and bringing together the critical success factors are enough to make you a successful private equity investor, but there are a few things that you can do to turn a good investment into an exceptional and rewarding life’s work.

Whether it is a successful mentor, proper capitalization, the right attitude, a large enough market, a good marketing plan, the ability to take action, an end result that will be worth the investment, a sound Plan B (hedge) or a workable exit, miss any one of these advanced items and your investment is far more at risk than necessary.

Investments versus Expenses

As a general rule, investments are things that make you wealthier or more productive. You cannot make an investment in a new TV or a new stereo; these items lose value after you purchase them and do not add to your wealth.

Investments are only worth going into debt for when they will increase your ability to make money. A new machine to manufacture goods faster falls in this category, as does an education that will enhance your ability to understand the nuances of a particular business.

This story is an example of investing in an education that will enhance your ability to make money.

I recently had a rewarding experience with a young person that I have assisted in gaining a college education over the past few years. This young woman has dedicated significant time over several years to pursue a college degree in Accounting. She scores at the top of her class, is Magna Cum Laude at her university and all in all a very successful student. She recently gained one of the most coveted internships and scholarships in her field of study, accompanied by a significant raise in pay.

We are talking the other day and she looked at me and said, "About a year ago, I set a goal to double my salary and today I finally realized that I would never have been able to do that without the education I am currently seeking."

What a revelation this was for her, to be successful she needed education in the topic she was to pursue.

The same is true about Private Equity Investing. To be successful, you must become highly educated in the investment topic, even to the point of being an authority on the subject. Furthermore, you must become educated in the competition for investment dollars.

Know When To Act

The ability to seize an opportunity has resulted in more successful investments than any other single activity in human history.

During the depression of the 1930s, my great-grandfather had a problem with boll weevils in his cotton crop. He tried everything to rid his crop of the pests. Nothing seemed to work.

One night, my grandmother recounts, he sat straight up in bed, and said "I've got it". The next day he climbed into his old pickup and headed for his cousin's metal shop in Stamford, Texas, some 90 miles away.

Over the next two weeks, my great-grandfather designed and built the pre-cursor to one style of cotton stripper. His idea was to blow air from underneath the plant using a mobile device that slid under the plants along the ground with wheels between the cotton rows. The moving air would blow the weevils into a bin and thus rid his crops of the pests. The invention worked wonderfully.

Recognize when to take action. Take action when opportunity presents itself.

He took his invention to several tractor manufactures. Because many farmers were battling boll weevils, he easily found a major tractor company to buy and patent his invention.

Great-grandfather cleared enough profit to quit farming, and buy some rent houses.

Because this poor dry-land farmer from central Texas took action when he reached the "Age of Awakening", he was able to retire in comfort and establish an income that would support his wife for her entire lifetime and his children for decades. He was also able to enjoy the remainder of his life without killing himself hoeing cotton.

"When is the best time to invest?" I get this question every day. This is not a difficult question to answer. My off the cuff response is "You can't win if you're not in the game". In my experience, it is not "when" you invest, today is always a good day to start, but how you invest, smart -vs- dumb.

I have interviewed hundreds of equity investors who consider themselves to be early-stage players. To them, an early-stage company has annual sales of $5 million or more. This is considered very early stage by Wall Street standards, but in the private equity world where I live and work, this is a large company. This is a perfect company that is ready to expand, acquire the competition, or be sold to a larger player, for a substantial profit.

Personally, I find gems in start-up companies who are working with next-generation ideas whose managers are thinking two curves ahead. In the 1970's, Bill Gates fell into this category.

In 2007, I did some preliminary research on a pipeline leak detection company who was using a new infrared technology to discover hydrocarbon leaks in refineries. You can imagine how valuable this technology is with natural gas at record high prices. Using very little imagination, the numbers become staggering quickly.

This rural Texas team has proven their technology many times over. They had recently grown their sales to $1,000,000 annually with a family staff of six. They had airborne technologies, hand held technologies, stationary applications, they were covering all the bases.

The principal owner of this company is a man about 50 years of age. He knows that he has a tiger by the tail, but isn't quite sure exactly how to proceed.

This company is a prime candidate for private equity capital, but only if the personality's mesh in the proper way.

A funny story about this company. This team was invited to a leak-detection competition against teams from places like MIT, Texas A&M, Lawrence Livermore National Laboratory, Argonne National Laboratory, Los Alamos, and NASA. All of these places have highly educated team members that are responsible for technology creation and management in the leak detection arena. You can imagine that vapor leaks are a major area of concern at places like NASA as well as any oil & gas refinery.

The invited teams met at one of the large refineries near Houston. The teams had a set amount of time to locate and identify leaks in the refinery. The refinery was divided into sections. Each team would work on each section at different times during the competition. The team that won the contest also won a multimillion-dollar contract to do leak detection in the refinery for a year.

The other teams, with as many as 12 highly trained members, showed up in matching jump-suits. They were Ph.D. candidates, led by Ph.D.'s with the nicest equipment that money could buy.

My friend's team of 4 had just completed a pipeline detection job in the field near Houston. They drove up in a muddy pickup. They were from a small Texas town, led by a high school graduate. They showed up wearing their cowboy hats, work boots, and overalls. They looked worn, but they were ready to go to work. My friend knew that no one in the competition had ever seen their technology.

The competition lasted two 2 days and was divided into 4 different work sessions. My friend's team, with their hand-made equipment, was doing a remarkable job of showcasing their technology.

At the beginning of the second day, a 50-something woman leader of one of the highly educated teams, looked down over her reading glasses at a high school age assistant on our rural Texas team and said, "you know this is a million dollar contract you are competing for?" The young man looked down shyly and said "Yes Ma'am". The lady smiled at our young assistant and said "You know you all are kicking our ass." The young assistant looked up, smiled broadly and said "yes ma'am." They both smiled.

The second-place team surveyed 750 connections per hour and found fewer than 200 leaks in 4 hours. The winning team, made of hard working technical people and family members, surveyed over 3,000 connections per hour and identified an average of 400 leaks in a four hour period, over the same competition area. The contract went to the simple yet competitive rural Texas team.

We are still considering an investment in this company, but the principal is just not ready. Who knows, he may never be ready.

The thing that attracts us to this investment is competitive advantage, new technology and simplicity along with a team of hard working, knowledgeable people who know how to get the job done.

Sustainable competitive advantage is one of the key elements I seek when evaluating a potential private equity investment. If the capital seeker is good at what they do (potentially a market leader), and if they have a competitive advantage either in information access, technology, market penetration and/or ambition, then you, the investor, should stop, look and listen because a potential deal is in the offing.

An example of information access/advantage is a recent research program we started. In our real estate group, we noticed that several newly developed areas of a large city were not being served by mini-storage facilities. We conducted research for a 24 -month period where we identified every existing or proposed/permitted self -storage facility in this metro area of 2 million people.

We spoke to each city and to local developers to determine the status of the markets. We visited each and every existing site. We studied the demographics of each location, the customer base, and the occupancy.

During this process, we uncovered several worthy properties that were for sale, but not being actively marketed. We conducted a preliminary financial analysis of the properties of interest. This was, by far, the largest private database of self-storage properties that we had ever seen for this marketplace. After we finished our field reconnaissance, when the database was plotted on a demographic map, we identified over 25 areas that were prime candidates for mini-storage facilities. This research has led us to several compelling investments that make substantial profits day and night, with no management from the investor and upside potential rarely seen. These are deals we like.

Let's Everybody KISS
(Keep It Simple, Stupid!)

KISS is the basic mantra for private equity investing. In my experience, the simplest investments are generally the best investments.

Filling an overlooked niche, making a product cheaper, giving a customer what they need, improving society, these are all worthy endeavors, but when an investment gets too complicated or acquires too many players, it generally means trouble and money wasted. Normally it is my money that is being wasted which is something I frown on considerably.

The recent sub-prime lending debacle of 2007-08 is a prime example of a simple idea getting out of control. For generations in the US, mortgages were handled in a very simple way, the borrower would prove his credit worthiness, he would save for the down payment and he would execute a mortgage when he was ready and able to service the obligation. The mortgage originators were very careful not to over-qualify a potential borrower because their reputations and money were on the line if the mortgage when bad. Often, they were under contract to purchase every non-performing loan back from the investors and collect the money themselves. The investor would purchase that mortgage, providing capital and profit from his investment. Clean, simple, workable and responsible.

During the time of easy money and market securitization from 2003 to 2007, the generators of the mortgage-backed securities were so caught up in making money and slicing every dime out of the mortgage pie, that they lost sight of the real financial risk and the needs of their customers (secure investments). Frankly, they committed fraud by not disclosing to their investors all the pitfalls of the mortgages they were writing. They also committed fraud on the rating agencies when they did not disclose the true strength of the borrowers. When mortgages began to go sour, the "promoters" (I call them part time mortgage brokers), who had gotten rich off of fees, were sitting on their yachts, drinking umbrella drinks, looking for the next big pigeon.

They had no personal stake in their reputations. They had no responsibility. There were no buy-back clauses in the contracts they had with investment houses. They had no reason to care if their investors were left in a terrible position. They were not responsible for the fraud they were committing because the market shielded them from their responsibilities. As of the writing of this book, many of them are finding out that they were indeed responsible and several of them are going to spend time behind bars for their acts of fraud.

Keeping it simple, in the private equity world, means avoiding people who do not add value, while working with people who are responsible. The best deals I have ever been involved with consisted of a small group of investors and one or two principal investees. Each party bringing their experiences, expertise, and value to the program. Each party knowing and executing their responsibilities as well as understanding the responsibilities of all other parties.

The investors knew the money-end and the business side of the program. The investees know how to execute and get the job done.

Simple and ideal,
Everyone working towards the same goal.
All parties doing the right thing the right way.

Building A Natural Hedge

Cutting corners during a startup or expansion phase is poor business practice and will hurt you in the long run. It takes a special type of investor to realize this because it is counter-intuitive. The wise investor will put a little more into the real assets required at startup to help secure his overall investment.

One thing that every investor can do to increase her chances of success is to have a workable "Plan B"; a back-up plan; a hedge against failure. Many industries lend themselves well to hedges and with the advent of a wide variety of derivative instruments in today's marketplace, hedging is getting easier all the time.

In the private equity world of "real assets" where I work, most hedges must be planned and created in the very beginning of the investment program.

For example, in our hospitality business, we build new hotel properties near major regional hospitals and universities. The natural "Plan B" for a hotel facility near a hospital is to become an assisted living facility if the hotel somehow does not perform. The natural hedge for a hotel near a university is to become a private dorm.

These are natural hedges. Our back-up plan will deliver our clients the necessary returns to meet their goals, when and if the original plan fails. To execute this hedge, we must plan ahead.

For example, when we construct our hotel facilities, they are all sprinkled as required, but we add additional wiring to accommodate the necessary systems for an assisted living facility. We build the doors wide enough; we build the bathroom access to easily be converted to handicapped for a small cost. These extra pieces cost a bit more in the beginning, but are well worth it in the overall picture.

What is good about this "Plan B" is that, due to the original location, near a regional hospital, the Assisted Living aspect of the property will often make more money than the original hotel development.

In the oil & gas world, the major uncontrollable risk is commodity price. In our analysis, we build in a hedging strategy that, during a market downturn, will assist the portfolio to return adequate cash-flow to the partners until the market can stabilize and recover.

Our hedging strategy, using simple marketable derivatives, is designed to return 10% on the investors' capital at a minimum during the worst of times. If the fund performs as expected, the returns will exceed 22% annually.

When you compare the downside of 10% profits in a down market, with the upside of greater than 22% returns in a stable market, the risk to the investor becomes extremely low. What is best about this investment vehicle, 22% is the expected return; the portfolio contains 100's of opportunities for extremely high upside potential, with many properties returning over 100% annually.

This type investment is the dream of the Private Equity Investor. You make money in the down markets, you make even more money in the up markets. Low downside risk with extreme upside potential, a dream come true for your portfolio.

For a startup venture the natural hedge is often the very first purchase, the office location and land. It is wise for an investor to consider paying a little more for the corporate space and owning it, not leasing it. If you position yourself correctly, you allow time and the markets to work in your favor, increasing the value of your property to enhance the returns from your business.

A wise move is to get slightly ahead of development with the purchase, then in 5-10 years when it comes time to sell, your land might possibly be the most valuable thing your company owns. If you look around any major city in America, you will see investors who started businesses 5 years ago on the outskirts of town, are now sitting on the most valuable piece of property in the market.

I cannot count how many times the initial investment in a good piece of commercial property has saved the investor when a private equity deal goes south.

Today, my company offices in a non-descript part of town where the property values have tripled over the past 10 years. Fifteen years ago, we invested in this parcel, knowing that someday we would want to build a hotel in this area. The right market timing rolled around about two years ago and my team has been designing and permitting a hospitality/retail complex to occupy a portion of the land that we own.

In the beginning, we purchased land for $.10 per square foot (10 cents). It was slightly removed from town, but near a large hospital and two universities. Today, Wal-Mart® and Cracker Barrel® have moved in and land sales in the area are well over $3.00 per square foot.

Regardless of how the hospitality program comes out, the original investors are very secure in this program, because the initial investment in land has appreciated handsomely.

Who To Invest In?

Someone with a workable vision who knows he doesn't know it all

It is generally a poor decision to invest in someone who is a Jack-of-all-trades, someone who tries to do everything himself, someone who does not know what he does not know.

Don't place your money with someone who doesn't have the focus and management skills to hire help when needed.

I recently listened to a conference speaker who was relatively computer-illiterate, but was netting over $100,000 per month selling products on the internet. His favorite saying was "I don't know the difference between a megabyte and a gigawhat, but I have people who do." This man knew what he did not know. He had people working with him who knew exactly what they were doing. He was a very successful private equity investor.

Private Equity investing is about finding someone who has the tools, the intelligence, experience, knowledge, education, and business savvy to succeed, but lacks the capital to execute.

The smartest investor on earth is the one who knows what she lacks and seeks out people who will help her succeed.

For me, an extremely smart equity investment is to provide financing to a management team who is doing the task, and simply needs capital to move to the next logical step. These types of businesses abound in the United States, Canada, and Northern Mexico. All they need is a helping hand to get off their knees.

One of the most successful venture business models in the modern world is known as the micro-loan program. Investors provide $100 micro loans to working people with the investment used to expand the workers business. The loan program is a tremendous success in developing countries and the repayment percentage is simply astounding.

I have a friend, Joe, who recently found success by backing someone who just needed capital and organization. Joe and his brother ran a very successful multimillion dollar business in the 1980s. They sold at the right time to a bigger company and then proceeded to make a series of poor investments until their money was gone.

Joe came across a prime example of a typical and safe private equity investment. The investee was a 40 something man who had been working for a medical device company for over 10 years. He was doing the job every day. The medical devices he had experience with were portable MRI and Ultrasound machines. This was a booming business at that time, and technicians who knew how to operate and repair the machinery were few and far between. The hurdles to entering the field were high with each machine costing upwards of $1 million.

This technician approached Joe with a plan. He personally knew the customer base from work with his current employer. He had the machinery research, the budget, the competitive set, the marketing plan, the technical expertise to operate and repair the equipment and everything else necessary for going into business. Everything except the capital. He was a perfect Private Equity candidate.

Joe did his due diligence on the players, and had his network of investors focus on this program. Joe and the technician established a company, funded two prototype mobile MRI/Ultrasound machines, and went into business with a staff of six.

The entire process took about six months to execute. Joe managed the office and the finances. The technician managed the field operations. The company was soon netting over $150,000 per month on a $500,000 cash investment after all overhead and equipment payments (the other $1.5 million was leased equipment).

This was a home-run in the private equity business. I was proud to see Joe do so well after so many failures.

After a few years, a catastrophic event happened as inexperience spoiled this program. The primary investor and majority owner in this company passed away. His family, who became partners by default, decided that the family's youngest son needed a job and could manage this company. Joe's management skills, they concluded, were no longer needed.

Joe kept his equity share, but since he was a minority partner, his income dried up immediately (the family decided to stop distributions of company profits until year-end which stopped Joe's income in a 30-day period). All-in-all, a very poor ending to an extremely successful investment program.

Think about investments in terms of your mortality and always make adequate arrangements in case of your demise.

Someone who had it all, once, and handled it well.

Veer away from the child who inherited his father's money and hasn't been successful on his own. Be cautious with the prima donna who once drew a big salary and thinks that making money is easy and expected.

Find people who are energized by their past successes. They know how to be successful and have a taste for success that can't be learned except from experience. There is something in human nature that makes people who have tasted the good life through their hard work and efforts, want it back once it's lost. There are several good things about this type of investee.

First, they have a burning desire to do well, build something and be successful again.

Second, they know how to be successful.

Third, you have the ability to research how they handled themselves and treated others when things went awry. You can find out if they were dishonest or if they were fair-dealing when the tide turned. Did they lose their sense of moral direction when their world crumbled or did they remain level headed and thoughtful, taking care of business when times were bad. The steadfast, fair dealers are the people you will find as the best partners to have.

I would not hesitate to go into business with my friend Joe if he came across another ideal private equity investee like the MRI/Ultrasound technician.

A Passionate Craftsman

It is always a pleasure to trade with someone who takes pride in their work. Someone who's work ethic is apparent. Someone who takes care of you, the investor, as well as they take care of their children and customers. When you find one of these diamonds in the rough, you should look at them with helping eyes.

I once approached a young man who built and installed replacement windows as a business. You could tell from his work that he took pride in making every job as perfect as it could be. He built everything to order, custom in every way.

This window maker was doing very well, with 12 employees, servicing several large government contracts and doing several million dollars per year in gross sales from individuals and small businesses.

His business had been growing steadily for about 5 years, then its growth went stagnant. It was apparent to anyone who knew the business that the entrepreneur was at his limits, working 12 hour days trying to run this business all by himself. It took a toll on his lifestyle and his health.

This small business was the perfect example of an investee who needed an attitude adjustment and capital to make a mind shift and to get on the expansion wagon again.

Proper Capitalization

Do you believe that Bill Gates could have created Microsoft® without proper capitalization?

Do you believe that Warren Buffet would be successful today without proper capitalization?

The overall answer is a resounding NO.

Proper capitalization is essential for translating good ideas into great successes. Nothing in investing is more important than access to capital when it is needed. Many strong ideas have failed because there was not enough money for marketing and selling the product or manufacturing the product after the product was sold. Of course, other factors like management and execution play a big part, but **without proper capital in the form of cash to pay the bills and sell the product/service, no idea can become a winner.**

Interpretation of the Dun and Bradstreet® data often suggest that 80% of small businesses fail within five years of startup. My experience is that small business fatalities hover yearly around 50%. If a business makes it up to five years and is making a profit, then the team must be doing some things right.

One of the lease risky business investments anyone can make is to provide adequate capital to an experienced management team with a vision and skills to grow a profitable company.

If a company has a good business plan or an innovative idea, and a management team that is experienced in making money, then the only risk is that they will not have enough capital to be successful. I call this the "Buffet" value investing model.

I once consulted with a mulch company. The original investment included pick-up of the raw materials, processing and delivering the finished product to the customer. Simple, clean, and profitable. Taking something for free and making it valuable.

These managers were making money; their investment was paying off handsomely. One of the things that made this program so successful was that the investors gave the managers access to capital to grow the business. The original equipment was running full-time at top speed. The trucks were busy from sun up to sun down. The company was making all the money it could make.

It just so happened that management saw an opportunity to purchase a competitor for a good value and double their production and profitability, virtually overnight. The competitor had a strong asset base that was fairly priced and a knowledgeable team. This was a wonderful strategic move that added much synergism to the existing business.

The purchase was financially out of reach for the current capital structure, more than doubling the company size. The investors called me in to consult on the acquisition. As the equity investors involved in the program, it was their responsibility to bring the necessary financial resources to the table and they wanted to know how to execute the acquisition.

After review, we arranged the capital and the company instantly became the market leader in its niche, while more than doubling the investor's profitability along the way. This was an excellent Private Equity investment and a very wise use of capital.

Inadequate Capital is the Number One Cause of Failure

I cannot say this enough.

It costs money to be in business and inadequate capital is the number one cause of failure for private equity investors.

> ***If the people executing the investment are unhappy, the man putting up the money stands to lose everything.***

Marketing takes money and without marketing, few businesses can be successful.

Because no one wants to work for free, management must make adequate money to feel they are being paid what they are worth.

Being in business in a meaningful way takes money for rent (office payments), telephones, utilities, and general overhead.

I have seen hundreds of stubborn investors who refuse to inject additional capital in a program to get an investee over a hurdle. These were nearsighted decisions. If the program was good enough to invest in the first place and it only needs a fraction of the initial investment to achieve success, step up to the plate.

Don't be afraid. Manage your fear and make the proper decision. Put stipulations on your additional capital, but give, loan, provide the necessary capital, it will save you thousands and make you wealthy.

Here's an interesting story about the psychology surrounding this stubborn streak that many investors harbor.

Time and time again, my father and I would argue about how much lease bonus to pay a landowner for a mineral lease. There were over a dozen times during our career working together where we walked away from millions of dollars of oil in the ground, just because he would not pay an additional $5 per acre for a mineral lease.

One example was in Howard County, Texas, where we were working to purchase leases in 1980. We had an excellent prospect outlined; the primary leases were open for the taking at a price of $60 per acre from the landowner. Everyone else around the prospect had leased their tracts to us for $50/acre.

My father refused to budge. It was $10,000 extra for the prime lease in the play. Well, another investor was not so stubborn. The prospect was finally drilled a few years later, discovering over one-million barrels of oil. We lost that deal over a lousy $10,000. Don't let your "better judgment" and greed (read: stubborn streak) stand in the way of executing the original plan.

Knowing how to adequately capitalize a business is a difficult decision. My rule of thumb is to allow the managers, whom I already trust, to tell me how much capital will be necessary.

Then I further set aside additional resources to assist when the unknown happens.

THE UNIVERSAL QUANDRY
HOW MUCH CAPITAL?

Without adequate capital, no business can succeed.

With adequate capital, almost any well thought out, well managed and thoroughly researched business can be successful.

With too much capital, a business is doomed to failure from the very first dollar.

A Good Marketing Plan Executed by a Dynamic Team

When I was in college if anyone said to me, "I am a marketing major," I would smile at them and think, *you like to party*. It was a standing joke at my school that if you liked to party, you needed to be a marketing major.

It was not until I owned my first business that I truly understood how valuable a good salesman is to any organization.

If you don't admire a good insurance salesman, then you don't understand sales. Anyone who can take that many *NOs*, often in very rude terms, and still keep pitching deserves all the respect and help you can give them.

The correct sales plan and the proper team to execute the plan are critical to success. Your sales team will make your operation a success.

Confidence in the ability of your team to execute the idea is essential. It takes more than just an idea; it takes a true understanding of how to execute.

The good private equity investor will understand the psychology of the players and what motivates them.

Marketing is not cheap and will gobble up considerable amounts of capital, but for you to be successful, marketing is a requirement.

If your successful sales people are not some of the most highly paid people in your organization, then you need to take a look at your compensation structure, because a good salesman is worth his weight in gold.

Case in point: I have a friend who spent 15 years as the chief salesperson for a smallish insurance company. As I said before, if you know anything about insurance, it is all about salesmanship.

This friend laid out a plan, hired a team and grew the company from $30 million to $900 million in assets in just a few years, strictly through salesmanship. He made the owners wealthy beyond their imagination.

His reward? An annual year-end bonus of $1000.

Needless to say, after 12 years of hard work and that type of abuse, he is no longer with that company.

There are many ways to execute a marketing strategy. The guerilla approach to marketing is by far the cheapest and is frequently very effective. There have been several excellent books written on this subject.

I will not take time to tell you about marketing strategies. Do realize, however, that it is, critical to identify your market and do it early.

And The Proper Attitude Is?

One of the easiest mistakes a novice equity investor can make is to worry about what other people in the investment program are making. I am not talking about the commissions paid to regular people for doing their work, but rather who is making money in the execution of the investment.

Let me illustrate my point. Successful people must feel they have the potential to earn what they are worth; that the life they are leading is equitable; that their voices are being heard; and that their expertise is being used to its fullest advantage.

Private Equity Investors recognize that if you surround yourself with successful people, generating and managing the programs, your investments will make more money than imaginable.

All the successful equity investors I know have the attitude that *I don't know everything I need to know about this investment, so I must surround myself with people who do, and I will listen to their experience.*

If you are a real estate investor, your most valuable people should all be making good money because they are making the deals happen. If they are making money, then you are making money.

If your broker is doing his job by bringing you good properties before they go on the market and by making closings go smoothly (a valuable service indeed), he should be handsomely rewarded.

Let people make money on you.

Your banker is making capital available so you can leverage your investment dollar. Hopefully they are making nice fees, which you should not begrudge them.

Your contractors are making money doing exceptional work for you, on-time and under-budget. If they are doing their jobs, they should be well-rewarded.

Not only is it the nice thing to do, it's mandatory: let people make money on you for services rendered and contacts provided.

I have a client/partner I'll call Bob who enjoys success in just about everything he touches. We have discussed at length his secret to success.

Bob frequently reminds me, "I surround myself with people who know what they are doing and I provide the capital and some meager management skills."

He recently uncovered a very under-served sector of the commercial real estate market. Recognizing the opportunity, he researched the situation and uncovered the right management team to lead the efforts.

This team was a struggling group of professionals with a wide range of talents and a burning desire to be independent of the employer/employee relationship.

Bob put this team on an equal footing with him and with one another. Each was given the power to do what they were experienced in doing, and Bob's investment was off to a roaring start.

In their first three years, all the projects the management team has completed have returned over 100% annually to the equity investors, including Bob.

Motivation

Motivation must be understood in any Private Equity investment. You want investees who place you on the same level of importance as themselves and their families. Don't invest with someone whose needs come above those of the deal and ahead of your own.

On the other hand, steer clear of the investor who places his money above everything else, to the detriment of the program and the management team.

Avoid the investor who will remove his support or critical capital just because its performance doesn't meet projections for one quarter. An investor who places his returns above all other issues isn't your best partner.

In order to be a real benefit to your investments, the investor must see more than monetary gain in the program.

Profiting From A Down Market

Savvy private investors are always ready for a market downturn. Vast fortunes have been made due to investors having the foresight to place money in the market when downturns occur.

The Savings & Loan debacle of the 1990s resulted in the formation of the Resolution Trust Corporation (RTC) by the U.S. government. Bargains abounded and astounding fortunes were created through the asset sales that followed. Properties purchased from the RTC for ten cents on the dollar are now worth 20 times their purchase price 20 years prior.

During the tumultuous oil bust of 1983-1986, assets were being given away just so the owners would no longer have to pay the notes or the taxes. Banks were forcing sales for $.10 on the dollar.

Down-turns in markets never last. The human spirit simply will not allow it.

One company with a bank as a partner was forced to sell over 1000 barrels per day of oil production for less than $4000 per daily barrel ($4,000,000). A true bargain in anyone's book.

A mere 20 years later, that asset base would be worth over $50,000,000 by all conservative estimates. A tragic experience for the borrower and the banker, but a tremendous investment by the buyer.

My teams are looking to take advantage of the sub-prime mortgage debacle of 2007 as well as the downturn in the airline business. Tremendous opportunities to make money are presenting themselves today and will continue for the next decade due to the tightening of credit and my investment partners shall be ready.

A Workable Exit

From the very beginning, this is something that every investor needs, a plan exiting the private equity investment profitably. Whether the exit is ever used is up to you and the other participants, but a workable exit needs to be established up-front.

A variety of exit strategies exist, such as, a sale, a liquidation, a competitor buyout, a management buyout, or a public offering and as an astute investor, you should give serious consideration to your exit strategy.

In today's world, the competitor buyout, the management buyout or a public offering are the three preferred ways to exit a private equity investment profitably. The liquidation is usually associated with a failed venture, although it can be a viable exit if planned correctly from the start.

Realize the exit may take as long as a few years as you wait for market cycles to come into favor again (commodity prices are a prime example).

Patience is the key to making money in these markets.

Because each exit is dependent on the markets and supply/demand issues, I will not elaborate further on this topic, except to say, the simpler the structure, the easier the exit can happen and the more profitable the exit will be.

It's Okay to Say No

Have you had someone say to you, "if I give you this phone number, I get 10% of the company?" If so, I hope you replied with a resounding, "No thanks!"

I can't over-emphasize this point, as a private equity investor, one thing that must be avoided at all costs are **Commission Chains.**

If you do nothing but make a phone call, then all you are worth is a DIME.

Commission chains simply take all the fun out of investing.

A Commission Chain occurs when one guy has a friend that knows a friend who knows Donald Trump's yardman. He says he can get you an introduction to Trump, but he gets a 1% commission on the deal if you succeed, and his friend, his friend's friend, and the yard man all get 1% each for the introduction. If this sounds complicated, it is, and, in my experience, it always leads to a poor deal. Don't waste your time in pursuit of this situation.

If someone brings me a deal or project and tells me that Joe Bob gets 5% and Harold gets 1% and LuLu gets a fee, and I, as the investor, am to pay all the bills, I shut the door right then. I'll tell them, "When your principal gets ready to access some smart capital and earn some serious money, have her call me."

I have had brokers who had the audacity to say to me, "if I give you this phone number, I get 10% of the company". If they say that to me, I laugh and say, "I think I'll pass".

Being a private equity investor for over 30 years, I can tell you that the quickest way to sour my attitude, or the attitude of any investor, and make me withdraw from a potential investment at the closing table is to pay some outsider a share of the invested amount (usually my money) for nothing but a phone call or an introduction.

Almost equally as dreadful is to have the deal actually come together and, at the closing table, discover the distribution of funds is going to a previously-unrevealed commission chain. To forgo the wasted effort and time that goes into a closing that never happens, the principals must be totally honest, lay out the program details, including the distribution of funds which almost always includes brokerage and finding fees.

If the principals agree, up front, to any fees and commissions, then all is well to proceed to the exchange. This is the time when negotiation skills are implemented and the principals and investors commitment to the program undergoes its first real test.

Generally, at this time in the dance, the investment is outlined, it is decided who gets what ownership and what part of the profits and the initial letter of interest is put to paper. Among people who have worked together before, sometimes this in the only paperwork necessary until funding, but frequently the next stage of details are outlined in a much more extensive document.

The biggest mistake on the part of the investee (the person receiving the investment) is to not be forthcoming and upfront with their side of the program. Hidden costs and omission of facts can queer a deal faster than any other item. Honesty is always the best policy when dealing with someone else's money. In our offices, we have a policy that "if a deal can't stand full and honest disclosure of all the facts, then we find another deal".

I should explain that the fees being discussed here are outside commissions and fees paid to third parties that have not added any value to the investment process. Fees paid to a normal real estate commissions, legal work or fees paid to registered investment advisors as part of their normal course of business are not the extra fees being discussed in this section.

My objection is to outside commissions/finder's fees/introduction fees paid to third parties who have not added any value to the investment process.

In my practice, I have a network of people who regularly feed me investment ideas and deals, market research, real estate properties, companies to purchase, and management teams to back. If one of their programs comes to fruition, they are normally right in the middle of the deal as part of the management team. If not, I make sure they are fairly compensated for their time and efforts. We never want anyone to work for free, but neither do we want someone to make a million when all they do is make a single phone call.

If someone is actually working diligently on a program, bringing experience, advising, researching and uncovering due diligence items, or spending significant amounts of time upon execution of a proposed investment, they should be compensated for their time, either through ownership or money. After all, their time is worth something to the program.

Pay what the job is worth.

In our offices, if a broker contacts us with a tip, a phone number, a package he has picked up, and/or a story that turns into an equity investment for our team, then they get a small compensation check for their time at closing.

If a broker brings us a full package on a proposed investment which he has had some hand in putting together or has spent time doing due diligence for our benefit, if the program comes to fruition, then he gets compensated for the amount of time and effort he has in the program.

If an investee comes to us with a plan, the data to support that plan, an execution strategy including an entrance, an operating budget, a management team, a marketing program, capital he has invested from his own pocket and all other necessary research including a proper exit strategy, then he gets an ownership interest commensurate with his level of due diligence, investment, effort and experience.

Its 10 O'Clock. Do You Know Where Your Money Is?

As a sound financial investor in private deals, it is your responsibility (and I contend it should be a requirement) that you understand where your dollars are going and who is benefiting from your investments.

This usually means a semi-annual visit to the operations' bookkeeper to review their practices.

If your chosen management team will not open the records to you, I suggest that it is time to find a different team. I have actually sold investments in management teams who began to think the seed capital I provided to get them started was unimportant, now that they were doing "so well".

A frank discussion of these attitudes is not pretty, but it generally serves the purpose to either extricate you or change the management teams' stance.

In my current management company, Farpoint Private Equity Advisors, each partner receives a monthly report on activities in their investments along with a monthly financial statement on the program. Our investors are able, upon 24 hours notice, to review our financial records, in our offices. Our financials are audited annually. We view this as a critical part of having satisfied investors.

You Can't Win If You're Not In The Game

I frequently meet people who are petrified of losing money. To be safe, they tend to keep their money in the bank, in certificates of deposit, and let the bank pay them marginal, frequently money-losing rates of return.

These investors don't understand that their dollars buy half what they did five years ago, mainly due to inflation. They don't realize they have to be active in the investment marketplace to maintain their wealth.

My grandmother lost her husband when she was only 40. She continued to work, save, and actively invest in real estate until her death at the age of 80.

Grandmamma bought and sold houses, fixed them up with the help of her sons, lived in them, rented them, and always sold them at a profit -- all with cash. Every time we had a serious family discussion, she'd remind us, *"If you're not an active investor, you're losing ground every day."*

Grandmamma didn't even finish high school, but she was surely wise.

I was talking to her one day and asked her about why she owned so many houses. Her kind and loving response was "I used to own an iron and an ironing board". What she meant by that was that she reached the Age of Awakening with an iron in her hand when she was about 30 years of age. At that point, she realized that her hard labor was never going to get her the life that she wanted by itself and that she had to make her money work for her as hard as she had worked for it.

Pitfall #1

GREED

I believe every man has a level of larceny in his heart that can surface at any time. The type of partners you want will be able to control this particular emotion. They will understand that what is best for the group will ultimately gain the results they seek for themselves. When all partners put what is best for the group ahead of what is best for them, everyone wins.

It is critical to be in business with people who have similar goals to yours, not people who are simply greedy.

I recently attended a venture forum in Houston. In the room were 12 venture capitalists and about 100 capital-seekers. The program allowed three of the seekers to make a 15-minute presentation about the merits and potential of their venture.

The second presenter was a nice looking black man in his mid-20s. He was wearing an Uncle Sam costume, complete with hat and whiskers. This college graduate had a degree in accounting and a CPA designation. His entire presentation was a 10 minute discourse on how he deserved to be rich and how the venture capital providers should assist him in creating a chain of tax preparation providers (like H&R Block®) to serve the poor, black communities around the U.S.

There was no discussion of need or competition. The market wasn't explained. No business plans came forth. Budget needs weren't mentioned.

The only statements that were made were about how the young graduate deserved to be rich, and the capital providers should give him money so he could live in a style he would like.

As he concluded his presentation, everyone in the room was laughing so hard they had tears in their eyes.

He didn't get the money.

Finding good private equity investments where everyone involved wins is not an easy task. It seems that there is always one owner or manager who has a greedy streak, and I refuse to do business with greedy people.

The old adage, *"Pigs get fat, hogs get slaughtered"* is one of the age-old truths surrounding good private equity investing. **Greed in direct investments will lead to failure.**

Be wary of words and phrases like *control*, *calling the shots*, *51%*, *if things don't work out*. The investor who uses these words might want such a high ownership in the project that the deal originators will not profit if the project reaches every success goal.

In this case, the original entrepreneurs could consider selling the idea to the capital provider, retaining a small ownership position in the finished project, allowing the private equity investor to be in control and risk his own money in his own project.

Odds are if the investor is that greedy, the entrepreneur will probably be able to purchase the technology back at a deep discount shortly after the deal is struck.

An example of what I am talking about: a major multi-national company was purchasing small businesses that had exceptional profit margins, folding them into the big company to increase profit margins by adding economies of scale, management and capital structure. This multi-national had acquired a certain small gasket-maker who was highly profitable.

The gasket-maker was just at the limit of what they could do as a small, owner-managed company.

The multi-national wanted control over the manufacturing processes, but the company owner held all the patents.

The clever owner decided to sell his company for US$100,000,000. He gave his employees a generous retirement and retained a handsome profit for himself. The multi-national began running the company and, before long, turned it into the largest money looser on their books.

Three years later, the original owner repurchased the company for $5,000,000. Most of his original employees returned to work with him, and he was off and running again.

Obviously, the multi-national could have invested wisely with this owner and still be in a very profitable business niche today, making 100% annually on their investment, but they were greedy. They wanted to call all the shots in a market segment where they knew nothing. I'll say it again: **greed leads to failure**.

A successful private equity investor understands that everyone in the program must win and does not mind if someone else makes money off of his investment, so long as he also makes the profits he is expecting. This private equity investor will own enough of the project that, if the investment succeeds, even in a marginal way, he will make a minimum threshold return on his investment.

This threshold is different for every investor because we all view risk differently. The amount sought by the investor will be commensurate with the amount of risk he faces in the marketplace and in other investment vehicles.

I am appalled by the number of unscrupulous businessmen who take staggering salaries from the profits of companies when the people who work for them make minimum wage. An ethical private equity investor will not support nor allow this circumstance to continue.

Pitfall #2
AMBITION

Of course, ambition is a requirement for any private equity investment to succeed, but too much ambition on the part of management can be harmful and lead to failure.

The people you are investing in must possess a healthy level of ambition. Otherwise, they may take your investment but stop moving to a higher and better position. Or perhaps they simply move on to other projects, leaving you in the unenviable position of locating competent people to operate your investment.

I have an acquaintance who is an accountant for a small college, working in the financial aid office. Every semester, one or two students apply for financial aid, stay in school just long enough to get their distributions of government grants and loans, empty their account, drop out and move on, never to repay the loans or grant monies they received.

Believe me, if I ever interview a person who has intentionally done something like this, I certainly won't be hiring or investing with them.

It's hard to pre-determine when ambition is at the appropriate level. Success in prior efforts can instill ambition in a person. Conversation about supporting a family and putting children through college are good signs in a manager/investee, as is talk about what you, the investor, will get out of the relationship.

An acquaintance had a graduating son who would soon need an income. The child had not worked during his college career, so he had no track-record of any type of work ethic. He made poor grades and just managed to graduate.

The son convinced dad, with typical youthful vigor and enthusiasm that the two should go into business together. Dad agreed, albeit somewhat reluctantly. He borrowed the money to purchase a franchise for his twenty-something child to own and manage on a daily basis. The books looked good, in the beginning, but the shop never reached those numbers.

He was hopeful that his chances for success had improved when the son jumped in at full steam. But the son stuck with it all of about 90 days.

Boredom soon set in and the son decided to move on to something else, leaving his father — his investor, as an absentee owner (he lived a distance from the property) with no responsible party able to assist him in running the business.

The son bailed out, unapologetically leaving dad to clean up the mess. His ambition had outpaced his ability to complete the task at hand. This type of ambition must be avoided at all costs.

Dad made a poor business decision which cost him thousands of dollars.

I have another acquaintance who, at first blush, appears to be the most ambitious person you will ever meet; however, he thinks about himself first, and he cannot close a deal.

He is constantly turning up projects that will make him wealthy, while only giving me my investment back with a savings account return. His ambition is misplaced. I will never enter into a deal with him. My investment would be at risk of total loss.

In the 1990s, when I worked for the US Environmental Protection Agency, we ran a program called "Meet the Money" where private investors were invited to hear entrepreneurs that had innovative environmentally friendly technologies and ideas. These entrepreneurs had 30 minutes to openly present their programs, the finances and make their request.

If the investors were interested, they would schedule a meeting to inquire further into the opportunity.

Time after time, these entrepreneurs would present passbook savings returns to these private equity investors, hoping that they would become excited about the opportunity.

This was a classic example of entrepreneurial ambition being out of sync with the real world.

Regrettably, it's all too common to find entrepreneurs who think about themselves first and the needs of the equity investor second.

Pitfall #3

IGNORANCE

In 1976, John Smith opened a clothing store in a small town in Tennessee.

In 2003, after hearing such hype about the Internet, Mr. Smith had a local kid develop a website for his store. They posted it on the web and sat back, waiting for orders. Nothing was done to promote the site and, three years later, the record showed no sales and few site visitors.

Now it was 2006 and his son, John Jr., had studied internet marketing in college. John Jr. told his father, "I'm going to sell shirts on the internet."

His father replied, "I've tried that; thc internet simply does not work".

John Jr. invested a few hundred dollars to launch and market his site. Within a year, he had doubled the sales from his father's store. All on the internet.

> ***Just because it does not work for you, doesn't mean it won't work for someone with a different skill set.***

As it turned out, the Internet did work as a sales tool for the one who knew how to use it. In this case, ignorance on the part of the dad led to failure.

The Kelly Snyder Oil Field of Scurry County, Texas, is a classic case of how thinking "if it doesn't work for me it won't work for you" can cost billions of dollars.

In 1948, a sleepy geologist working for Humble Oil was drilling through 200 feet of rock he did not recognize. The shows of oil were intermittent and inconsistent, and there was no oil production nearby from that depth.

He was focused on the company's objective, a deeper horizon, and didn't realize the value of what he saw. On his advice, Humble plugged the well.

Two years later, Standard Oil obtained the rights and re-entered the well. They made it into a producer and went on to extend the Kelly-Snyder field several miles. The Standard geologists saw shows of oil, porosity and production within 15 miles of the location and in their mind that meant success. The geologists at Humble had a totally different opinion, which caused them to pass up the opportunity of a lifetime.

Today, this billion-barrel field contains over 1600 producing oil wells, and produced over 210,000 barrels of oil per day at its peak.

This field, initially dismissed by the best of professional oil finders, remains one of North America's premier oil discoveries of the 20th century.

A 100-room motel was built in the 1940s on the main thoroughfare between Dallas and Los Angeles. It was a great success in its heyday.

Over the years, the motel changed hands several times and became less successful. As market forces changed and as the various owners didn't keep up with innovations and maintenance, the property fell to the bottom of the market.

Then, in 2000, a new owner purchased the facility with a vision for success and the appropriate amount of capital. He paid attention to the business and was a master at the details that make for successful hospitality. The building was spruced up; the lawns were manicured; the pool was repaired and painted. The restaurant, reception area, bedrooms, and baths were remodeled.

Today the old motel yields well over 30% on equity yearly. The owner has further parlayed this initial success into a venture that includes at least five additional properties, all doing well in their own right.

You are probably familiar with the story of FedEx®, whose founder, Fred Smith, tried and failed several times to launch the innovative idea of overnight package delivery into the marketplace.

He was frequently undercapitalized.

He was told how it needed to be done by people who did not share his vision for success. He was not allowed to execute his plan, the way he knew it needed to be executed…all which led to failure after failure.

But Mr. Smith kept trying. He continued working the idea until someone with the proper vision and capital stepped up to the plate.

Today, FedEx posts revenues over $36 billion annually, delivering over 6.5 million packages a day.

Another example of how ignorance leads to failure is my youthful run at a commercial real estate development. As a young and eager investor, I lived two hours from a population center of 4,000,000. In my hometown, at the intersection of two major highways, 100,000 cars passed by daily. I thought my location was absolutely ideal for a regional outlet mall and entertainment center.

I personally invested several thousand dollars in the initial stages of the development plan, including renderings, feasibility studies and construction budgets. I took my package and scheduled meetings with several national outlet mall managers about locating in my area.

In one of my meetings with the largest outlet mall management company in America, the company's CEO looked me in the eye, and said "Paul, I appreciate your research and presentation, but you just don't have the market to support even a small facility."

He proceeded to outline the demographics that made an outlet mall work and, to my surprise, he was right, and what he said made perfect sense.

Ignorance of the facts is a major pitfall in the Private Equity Investing world.

I did not have even half the necessary market with the right income structure to make my planned development work. My plan was a waste of time and money, and this man knew it.

That day I learned not to argue with a man who has superior information and experience. Once I recovered from my disappointment, this was a major breakthrough in my education about investing in private equity.

He very kindly educated me and I remain grateful for this education to this day.

Pitfall #4

ELEVATED EXPECTATIONS

Reality is **never** going to match up to expectations when plans aren't established in a realistic framework using numbers from an actual company or the experience of someone who has executed the plan before.

In the private equity world I know, the daily rule of thumb is the One-Quarter Rule (also known as the **40% Lie**).

If a novice comes to you with a plan and a budget, multiply their expense numbers and time frames by four to get a more accurate view of how long the project will take and how much it will actually cost.

The 40% Lie is a pitfall that every investor has fallen into if she has been investing for any period of time.

In short, take whatever an income producing asset is quoted as making, subtract 40%, and you will probably be pretty close to the truth. This is not to say that people who are selling projects or businesses are liars, they are just the eternal optimist.

It is human nature to be optimistic.

The presenter knows that the property has produced $xx for one month or one year in the past, and they fully believe this elevated income stream is the true and consistent value of the business on the selling block.

***Humans are naturally OPTIMISTIC.
Be Careful of the 40% Lie.***

If you invest totally on what the seller is presenting, without doing your due diligence, you will end up broke and unhappy.

Beware the Slam Dunk

My friend, Sally, met her Waterloo at a daycare.

In the 1970s and early 1980s, in many West Texas towns, Texas Instruments® built assembly plants and put rural Texans to work building calculators and watches. TI viewed these underutilized labor forces as a source of cheap labor and for several decades the program was very successful.

Sally's story begins there.

The majority of the workers in these assembly plants were single mothers with young children. They welcomed the well-paying TI jobs which provided the resources to raise their families.

Sally worked at one of the plants, and made a personal study of the environment. She realized that 500 single working mothers, most with small children, were working eight-hour shifts on a campus they couldn't leave. They needed affordable daycare at or near their workplace so they could visit their children during the day.

My friend approached the plant about setting aside a room for an on-site daycare center at a reasonable lease rate. The management liked the idea.

Sally would provide all the renovations, all the licensing, all the personnel, all the necessary equipment and transportation to and from school. She would own the business and lease space from the plant.

She had great plans and envisioned that someday, each TI plant would have one of her daycare facilities as part of the plant.

After $100,000 in expenses, paid from her retirement plan, Sally opened her doors to the plant workers.

Human nature is hard to judge, tough to plan for, and difficult to manage.

Everything went smoothly for a few months as the center cared for 150 kids a day. Then some of the lower-paid mothers began paying a week or two late; then others were two to three weeks late, then a month late.

Soon, Sally was dipping into her 401K to meet payroll. Over half of the customers stopped paying for the services as agreed. This all happened within a nine-month period.

Sally needed a minimum of 75 paying customers to make the program break even. Anything below that, she was losing money every day.

What she didn't anticipate was that the plant workers began to look upon the daycare as an "entitlement" program. They began to resent having to pay for the service. They began to believe that because they were working hard for TI, the company should provide the daycare.

Sally's investment — seemingly a slam-dunk — went terribly awry due to human nature. There was nothing she could do other than salvage what he could from the assets and close down. This was a terrible education, and she is still recovering from this mis-step 20 years later.

Pitfall #5

OVER-CONFIDENCE

In the 1990s, I knew a man who spent tens of thousands of dollars to build and equip a new store in a regional mall. This dessert and coffee shop needed to make gross monthly sales of $15,000 to break even.

> ***Your WILL to make a project work won't overcome the facts.***

Given the market he was serving, $500 per day in gross sales on coffee, ice cream, and pastries seemed like a small hurdle.

Five years earlier, a friend of mine had owned and managed a similar store in the same mall, serving the same types of products. His store was smaller and needed sales of $7,500 per month to succeed. The store was well managed, but could only average sales of $6,000 per month.

My friend relayed his experience to the owner of the new store, but his comments fell on deaf ears. The new owner was so entranced with his dream of success that he couldn't clearly look at the numbers and facts being presented.

My friend openly shared what he had learned about the buying habits of the patrons, the price points they would stand, the products they would buy, and the frequency of purchases. These facts indicated that the new store would not even come close to making the needed income.

The new owner went ahead with the business. The store performed exactly as experience had predicted, almost to the dollar. The store lasted less than 18 months, and the new owner and his partners lost their entire investment plus some.

Take heed when someone, armed with experience, facts and figures, shows that your idea lacks a critical success factor.

Pitfall #6
MARGINAL DEALS

One of the most crushing feelings anyone can have in life is to learn that all their hard work, all their sleepless nights and dedication, their years of investment, effort and sacrifice are not worth the end result.

I once knew a young man who left Texas, drama degree in hand, to work on Broadway. After all, that is every stage person's dream, be a big star on Broadway. Working on a hit Broadway show is the pinnacle, the ultimate, the brass ring.

After 7 years of mind-numbing work, struggling to pay his rent, he finally landed a position as an executive on one of the highest-rated productions on Broadway. After opening night, he looked at his life, his shared one room apartment, and his salary that was not enough to allow him to ride the subway.

Then and there he concluded his lifestyle at the top of the Broadway scene was not at all what he expected. He decided it wasn't worth the sacrifices he had made to get there.

The next day, he packed his bags and moved out of New York and on with his life.

I have an associate, who I greatly respect for his wisdom in the public markets and in particular, the creation and administration of qualified retirement plans for wealthy clients. At this, he is one of the best I have ever met.

We were discussing private investing one day and he says to me "you know, I bought a franchise."

I looked at him and said, *"Why in the world would you do that?"*

He said, "I thought it was a good idea, after all, the franchise support is there to help us."

I cringed.

My friend, whom I greatly respect, had fallen into one of today's biggest business traps, thinking that a franchise company will be there to assist him when his investment goes awry.

What was most frustrating of all was that, if this store had performed as the very top of the marketplace, created the most sales in the State for a store of its kind, it would only return 12% on his equity, not nearly enough to support the risk that was undertaken by this $200,000 investment.

Why would you toil in a marginal deal that, from the very beginning, will not pay you or your people for the time and effort?

All- in-all, this was a very poor decision on the part of my friend. **Lesson: Do not invest in marginal deals.**

Don't invest your time and money unless success will meet your expectations.

In our world of private equity investing, the absolute minimum expectation is a 20% annual return on invested capital, without leverage, for the safest investment we can make. My firms' typical private equity investment is designed to yield 50% annually.

Pitfall #7

COUNTING ON THE GOVERNMENT

Having worked for years on both sides of the street regarding investments that rely on the government, my experience tells me that projects that are solely based upon government programs or subsidies are, more often than not, a poor investment. If a potential investee approached me with a gap in a government program as his main support for investing in a venture, I don't hesitate. I don't even listen. I quickly say "no thanks!"

The same rule applies to so-called "tax shelters." If the IRS leaves a loophole you can take advantage of when no one else can, watch out. My experience with "tax shelters" is that the investor spends more time and money in court trying to protect his position while the attorneys make all the money.

I don't have any "tax shelter" investments in my private equity management practice. I take the cream-of–the-crop investment opportunities, set them up in the most tax-advantaged way possible, execute, and then pay the taxes that are legally due. And we still outperform all published market indexes on a regular basis.

When I was with the Environmental Protection Agency in Dallas, I found it remarkable the number of people who would thumb their noses at the government, usually out of arrogance.

This isn't smart, because when the government wants to act, they can put your face in the mud and not let you breathe without permission.

I know of several cases where "bad actors" were audited and inspected more than once a year. They spent millions of dollars defending themselves against the most mundane charges. What a waste of time and life, especially when their activities were hurting the health and welfare of potentially thousands of individuals.

This is not to say that taking government research and exploiting it is not a good idea. It is a wonderful moneymaking idea. But if you get into an investment program that depends on continued funding by the government or tax advantages from the government to be successful, you are in the most perilous of circumstances.

Some government programs are better than others. HUD (Housing and Urban Development) programs that lend money or pay rent for poor and elderly populations are some of the more stable programs.

It is certainly wise to apply for every grant and subsidy available, but I never participate in a program that, to be successful, is solely dependent on a government loophole, grant or loan. I also suspect every investment program that must rely on government tax benefits or tax incentives to be profitable.

If your sole profits come from a government agency, then you are at great risk of losing your entire investment.

The government has no heart or emotion when it comes to you and your profits. The people who administer programs and vote in Congress have absolutely no loyalty to you, regardless of how much money you have donated to them or how hard you have worked in the past.

A prime example is the Supercollider project in Texas.

In 1988, Congress voted several billion dollars of government money to build a Supercollider in Ellis County, just minutes south of Dallas.

This project was a boom for the State, which was still recovering from the oil bust of 1984. Literally thousands of skilled and unskilled personnel were hired to dig a giant tunnel in the ground.

From the very start, this was a classic boondoggle. Billions were spent and made, but when the merry-go-round stopped, thousands of people lost everything they had worked so hard to amass and save.

When I consulted and worked for the EPA, I personally knew hundreds of former Supercollider employees. They had experienced one of the worst layoffs (termed a "reduction in force") in government history. These people had to find new jobs and start life over again at half- and even one-quarter pay, living in rent houses, surviving paycheck to paycheck because the windfall that was to last forever was over.

As an investor, this is not the kind of end result you want — not for you and not for the people who work with you or their families. Unless you make your living servicing the government, my recommendation is that you, as the intelligent investor, should never get involved with such an endeavor because you are setting yourself (and all your people) up for disaster and financial failure at the whim of someone with no heart.

NOTE: This section is not discussing Government Contracting as a business. If, as a company or investor, you can contract with the government for products and/or services to supplement your already-existing business, then this should certainly be done; but building a business solely on government handouts or loopholes is a poor and risky business model at best.

Pitfall #8
MISMANAGEMENT

I cannot venture a guess at the number of business failures that can be attributed to mismanagement or micro-management. The numbers are staggering.

I have an acquaintance whose family owned one of largest and most successful new car dealership in the United States. They sold and serviced more new cars over five decades than all the other local dealerships combined. One of every two cars on the roads of their community came from this dealership.

These men were masters at public relations and management and their operation made staggering profits.

Their secrets: exceptional customer service, fair dealing, hard work, and hiring the right team members to serve their customers. In turn, their dealership became one of the top in the country.

After a long and successful career, it came time for the owners to retire. The eldest son was poised to take over. The son gathered a few financial partners and purchased the dealership, keeping the name and all the goodwill that went with it.

Things rocked along for a year, profits were not as much as expected, but the partners thought they were in good hands because the son had "years of experience" in the management of this car dealership.

Year two rolled around and profits were down considerably. Sales were low and expenses were high. The equity partners were infusing capital they never expected to contribute.

This was a very bad sign for a business that was supposed to be profitable and cash-flowing (a cash cow as the son described). The partners began to worry about the ability of the manager to produce profitable results.

Upon investigation, it turns out that the son was a poor manager who sat in his office all day with the door closed. He did no public relations and did not meet a single customer.

He counted on others to buy and sell used cars for the used car lot. He did not visit with wholesalers or his retail staff. He did not monitor his service department. His new service people were young and rude. His sales people were greedy and rude. His used car people were dishonest and getting wealthy under the table.

The bottom line is that he did none of the things that made his predecessors successful, and his financial results didn't hide the facts.

Within three years of the son's ascension, his financial partners were frantically seeking a way to recover some of their investment. The dealership lost its franchise and 50 years of hard work and reputation were gone, never to be recovered. What was worse than the lost reputation was the equity investors' capital was lost, never to be recovered. And what was even more disappointing were the customers that had been very satisfied with the care and service for decades, now having to find a new dealer that they trusted.

Just because someone has 'been around' a successful business, they don't necessarily have the know-how to make money in that business.

Mis-management can quickly kill a business.

Next to capitalization, management is by far the most important aspect of a successful investment.

A few decades ago, one of my consulting clients was perhaps the world's worst micro-manager. This man had no clue about what it takes to be successful. He was impatient, rude, inconsiderate, and generally a very unlikable person.

What was humorous was that he was attempting to open and operate one of the most people-intensive businesses on earth, a minor emergency clinic. A business that must be operated by someone who enjoys helping people. Someone who cares about how people feel and how they are treated.

Smart people do stupid things every day, but being ignorant of what is required is totally inexcusable and the fastest way to lose *money.*

This client, a physician, was the typical know-it-all who really knows nothing of the practical world. He had worked in a hospital environment his entire career, where everything that he needed was supplied, just for the asking.

In his quest for higher profits and an early retirement, he had made a major capital investment from his retirement plan into building a minor emergency clinic. Instead of purchasing an ongoing business, he chose to build the business, facilities and all, *from scratch*.

This investment was one of the most poorly-planned and unwise decisions I could imagine. What was this guy thinking?

If you know anything about this type of operation, money is made through repeat customers. And customers return based on how they are treated. Treat patients well, they will come back and make you money. Treat them poorly and they (and their friends) will stay away, finding other physicians to pay.

As I mentioned, this physician was the worst micro-manager imaginable. He set the most unworkable deadlines I have ever seen in my 30 years as an investor/advisor.

He attempted to manage all the operations and renovations himself.

He worried about every penny he was spending.

He was resolute about opening the operation within two weeks of leasing his space (which needed major renovations).

Worst of all, he was computer-illiterate (which astounded me).

All-in-all, this was a very poorly planned operation led by someone who felt he needed no assistance.

What he failed to realize was that he lacked the skills to execute and be successful by himself.

A fatal flaw at best.

The investment was doomed from the very first penny, but no one could tell him, he simply wouldn't listen. The clinic finally opened after six months and at three times the original budget.

During those first months, every time I saw this doctor, he looked like he was about to have a stroke. His hair was disheveled, his face was red, his eyebrows were crinkled; he was a wreck, screaming at everyone around him like a maniac.

There were days when the clinic didn't have a single patient. Less than a year later, the clinic was closed.

The physician lost his entire investment and eventually took a job in an emergency room at an area hospital. The last time we spoke, 20 years after this fiasco, he was still trying to recover from the financial loss.

Debt: The Hidden Partner

A group of physicians recently convinced themselves that they would be better off owning their own hospital.

The lead doctor was a charismatic personality. He gathered 30 or so investors. He hired the best consultants he could find, but none of them had ever run a startup hospital before.

This new startup company borrowed millions and built a beautiful facility, opening with great fanfare.

The hospital limped along with marginal results and the management was soon forced to cut staff, below the Medicare minimums.

Then a tragic thing happened.

A patient died during a routine procedure. There was no one on-site to revive the patient, and the Emergency Medical Services ambulance had to be called.

Consequently, the hospital lost its Medicare designations and was forced to close.

At last review, the partners are now servicing the debt that was created, causing them terrible hardship.

This story was made possible by unsatisfactory capitalization, inferior management, and a poorly executed plan—exacerbated by the hidden partner, debt.

The feelings of giving a property back to the lender are those of failure, betrayal, and disappointment. Some people never recover from this circumstance.

But, even worse, to continue to pay a bank payment on a business gone is futile and gives you a sinking feeling in the pit of your stomach with each payment.

Most private equity investment funds use leverage to pump up their returns. While this makes for great marketing materials and a wonderful elevator pitch, the use of debt introduces a risk factor into the mix that is *very dangerous.*

I advise against the use of debt in private investing because one of the primary things that makes an investment successful is for all the partners to work in harmony with no excessive greed upon anyone's part.

When a bank gets involved, the harmony and synergism that make an investment successful become skewed. All the partners are not on the same page.

The bank has a different agenda that, when things get tough, will <u>never</u> mesh with the agenda of the business owners. Your individual banker may want to help you succeed and be profitable, but the bank board and regulators don't care if you are successful. The bank simply wants its principal returned with interest.

Banks, as an institution, are very near-sighted and lack any ability to care beyond a certain point. That point is generally the next earnings statement.

A client of mine built a wonderful company. He serviced his debt, repaid his loans on time, and the bank was happy to see him walk through the door…during the good times.

Then the economy turned, as it always does. This man had assets, income, and cash-flow, but not enough to service his bank debt. The market turn was temporary (as they always are), but the bank wouldn't wait. They foreclosed and sold the assets for twenty-five cents on the dollar.

The market did recover and, today, the assets are worth ten times what the loan value was (in less than five years) but my friend was ruined and is still recovering.

The banker lost; the bank board lost; my client lost; everyone lost because the bank's agenda was different from that of my client and his investors.

Due to this inequity, I advise all private equity investors to use debt sparingly and with extreme caution. Once the investment program is prospering, then the use of debt to enhance returns is a valid option, but not before and definitely not at start-up.

The general rule of thumb in the private equity world is when you can show and sustain $1.5 million in net profits for a sustainable period of time, then you might consider the use of debt in a limited way.

There are a few exceptions to my **No Debt!** rule.

When a company has adequate cash-flow and assets to more than cover a debt payment and the borrowed funds are needed to invest in new equipment that will make the business more profitable, then a meager amount of debt might be considered.

Debt is also acceptable in real estate investing, where it is virtually required. We use marginal debt in our real estate investments.

In my opinion as an equity investor, it is better to own 100% of a rental property that returns 18% on your money yearly and have the where-with-all to call the shots on the investment in a market downturn, than to own 25% of an investment that returns 25% and have debt as your partner.

As a private equity manager that works in the high yield marketplace, this policy allows me to sleep at night and prevents me from having to give my partners and investors bad news.

The Value of Review
or
How I Learned About Fraud

When I was in my 20s, I purchased a small restaurant. The prior owner's numbers showed acceptable annual performance that would make me a 15% return on investment.

Too late, I learned that he had "cooked" the books, inflating the store's income and misrepresenting the expenses (he hid some of the expenses in his other stores).

This was a fraudulent transaction from the very beginning, but I didn't realize for at least a year as I tried my best to make the numbers match the projections, while injecting thousands in extra capital.

In hindsight, my pre-purchase research was shallow and a horribly naïve. I took the financials as factual, since they had been prepared by the sellers' accountant. I learned later that the accountant did not audit the firm nor verify the numbers as they prepared the income tax returns and financial information. They simply accepted the seller's checkbook and self-reported sales figures as correct.

> ***Business is hard enough to execute profitably when your information is valid, much less when it's not.***

I should have asked about the process. Since this was a cash business, the risk of fraud was high, as I later learned.

I should have at least conducted my own audit, which would have only taken a few days.

The investment of a week or a few hundred dollars would have saved me thousands of dollars, and many sleepless nights.

Imagine for a minute that I am interested in that same restaurant, but the time is today instead of 30 years ago.

I will hire a team to review the purchase before anything is finalized. Sure, I will spend $5000 for the review, but I will save $100,000 because the review team will reveal the inaccuracy of the financials provided by the seller and his accountant.

A satisfactory team includes a qualified accountant (specifically one with experience in the business being acquired), an attorney who knows the right questions to ask, and an advisor familiar with the business type who can spot holes in the presented information.

Many investors are reluctant or too tightfisted to pay for a review. I've learned the hard way that this is the best money I can invest. Your due diligence should include a review team; at the very least, learn the procedure and conduct a thorough review yourself.

If you aren't prepared to pay for appropriate research, either in money or time, then be prepared to lose your investment.

If you are steady in your investing, eventually your experience will rule your judgment. At that time, you will instinctively discern a good program from a poor one.

Don't give up hope. Skills like this can only be taught through practice.

After 30 years of private equity investing, I feel that I have the experience and knowledge to see through the fluff and discern when a program makes sense, where the holes are, whether the deal has the makings of a profitable program or not.

Using my experience, I can have a five-minute conversation about an oil and gas property and determine if it is worth pursuit.

After over 15 years in the environmental and recycling business, it is not difficult to determine where the holes are in a recycling, reclamation or waste to energy program.

After 25 years in the real estate business, it is not difficult to tell when a program that is being proposed is over-promoted, unreasonable or bogus.

In the private equity business, experience is a major asset. That is why we require some type of mentor program for new people.

Seredipity?
or
Savvy Investing!

It's an exciting thing when ideas, management and capital merge together in just the right combination, creating the perfect investment vehicle. In the combination, if one of the elements is even slightly counterproductive, the resulting impact is only ordinary. Finding the right pieces and fitting them together to creating something extra-ordinary is rare and fantastic.

Bill Gates had a vision to create the personal computer operating system. The result was Microsoft®.

Henry Ford gathered his laziest workers and had them design the best and fastest way to assemble an automobile. The assembly line was born.

At my management company, you won't find high-tech, flash-in-the-pan investment ideas. We do not participate in bubbles. We are "core business" private equity investors seeking revolutionary ideas and every day products and services in which to invest. We look to invest in underserved markets with sound, hard assets where we can add value and create cash-flow.

In 2008, several areas have piqued our interest as having extraordinary potential.

With much of our country's population retiring to the country, **clean water** is in very short supply. We predict that drinking water will be in high demand over the next five decades. The person who owns the water systems, the infrastructure, and the water rights will reap untold profits.

The area of **commercial food resources**, being involved in a commodity-growing, food-processing, or transportation business, should see strong growth and profits over the next 50 years.

With traditional energy sources setting new cost highs, **alternative energy resources** including wind and solar, are quietly becoming an excellent place to invest.

As the energy markets fluctuate wildly, my long term view is that demand will continue to exceed supply into the future. We are seeing major shifts in this portion of the energy sector. Intelligent, clever **Oil and Gas** producers have made a 500% return on their investments in the last 10 years. We actively research opportunities in this arena. One operator I know turned a $3.5 million investment into $27 million in five years' time.

More capital goods being imported and transported to more affluent populations equals dramatic growth in **transportation resources** such as rail, trucking, and air cargo.

With 76 million customers in the US reaching 60 years of age in the next 15 years, anything involving **medical technologies and services** are a great place to invest.

These are just some of the areas where our interest is currently focused, but we interview teams and do research continuously to uncover opportunities.

Come join us and help make dreams come true.

Be sure to watch for our next publication

Winning With
Private Equity
II

Call me with your stories, trials and tribulations.

I will include them in my next book.

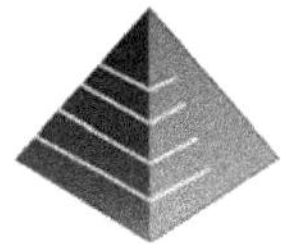

Paul A. Thomas
Farpoint Private Equity Advisors & Managers
PO Box 2677, Abilene, Texas 79604
558 Ambler Avenue, Abilene, Texas 79601
www.farpointadvisors.com
325.695.1329

www.ingramcontent.com/pod-product-compliance
Ingram Content Group UK Ltd.
Pitfield, Milton Keynes, MK11 3LW, UK
UKHW020138250726
13967UKWH00002B/739

9 781425 186753